D1616461

SEP :

FRUIT BOX LABELS

A COLLECTOR'S GUIDE

GORDON T. McCLELLAND

AND

JAY T. LAST

HILLCREST PRESS, INC. BEVERLY HILLS, CALIFORNIA

Hillcrest Press, Inc.
P.O. Box 10636
Beverly Hills, California 90210

Printed in the United States of America by California Lithograph Co.
Bound by National Bindery Co.
Photography by Sycamore Studios

TABLE OF CONTENTS

The colorful paper labels used for many years to identify and advertise wooden boxes of fruit now attract the attention of collectors, who are interested in them for their decorative and historical values. A variety of these small posters still exist in large enough quantities that collectors can acquire them at reasonable prices. This book classifies and illustrates over 1400 examples of this vibrant form of American commercial art.

INTRODUCTION

With the completion of the transcontinental railroads in the 1880's it became possible to ship western agricultural produce to midwestern and eastern markets. Fruit, which had remained unpicked in western orchards due to lack of demand, suddenly became commercially valuable, and a new industry developed.

The first products shipped were oranges and lemons from southern California, grapes from central California, and apples and pears from northern California, Oregon, and Washington. As railroad refrigeration techniques became more sophisticated, perishable produce such as melons, lettuce, and tomatoes also were shipped. A complex packing, shipping, and marketing network was developed to transfer this wide variety of western agricultural produce to eastern consumers.

The fruit box label was developed to identify and advertise these products. This colorful small paper poster was pasted on the end of the wooden box, serving as the means of communication between the grower and customer. Tens of thousands of labels were designed and used on billions of boxes until the 1950's, when wooden boxes began to be replaced by cardboard boxes with pre-printed label information. The paper labels, nearly all designed and printed in San Francisco and Los Angeles, serve as a historical record of California commercial art, and are of increasing interest to collectors.

The labels of primary interest to collectors today are those which were never attached to boxes. Small quantities of unused labels have been obtained from printers' archives, salesmen's sample books, and trade association files. The primary source of labels, though, is from unused packinghouse stocks. Because the shift from paper labels on wooden boxes to cardboard boxes with preprinted images was rapid, large quantities of paper labels remained unused in many packinghouses. In the past two decades, these labels gradually have been gathered up and now form the body of material available to collectors.

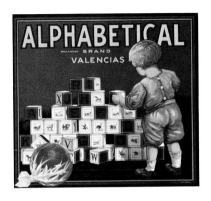

1. Label Title

2. Approximate label age. Successful designs often were used for many years. The date given is the period when the label was first designed and put into use.

3. City where the fruit was grown, packed, or shipped.

4. Label prices. These are established by the combination of the rarity of the label and the intrinsic interest of the label design and subject. Although no fixed prices for labels exist, an indication of the current label valuation is given by the following star system.

Blank Under $5
* $5–$25
* * $25–$50
* * * Over $50

Revised 1991 Price Guide

Blank	**$5-$10**
*	**$10-$45**
**	**$45-$100**
***	**Over $100**

CALIFORNIA ORANGES

California oranges were first grown in Los Angeles, Riverside, and San Bernardino counties, with later extensions to San Diego, Orange, and Ventura counties, and the central California San Joaquin Valley. A great deal of experimentation took place to find suitable growing areas and varieties of oranges for successful commercial production.

The growers finally settled on two varieties—the Navel orange, sweet, seedless, and juicy, an ideal orange for eating, available from December to late Spring; and the Valencia orange, good for both juice and eating, available from Spring to late Fall. California, therefore, has a citrus product available for sale the year around.

Oranges were shipped in wooden boxes from the 1880's until the 1950's, when cardboard boxes were introduced. The same box size and label format was used for this entire period. The label was about 11″ x 10″, in some cases with an additional ½″ strip on the top for packing information. The label was an ideal size and shape to present an attractive graphic image for product identification and advertisement. In the seventy year history of the use of wooden orange boxes, over a billion labeled boxes were shipped.

Because of the need to communicate with customers throughout the country, the orange marketing industry became highly organized, with individual growers combining into large packing and shipping organizations. Most of these growers cooperatives eventually joined one of the three large marketing organizations—Sunkist Growers, Mutual Orange Distributors, or the American Fruit Growers. These organizations became prominently featured on the labels.

In the early 1900's a grapefruit industry developed in California and Arizona. Grapefruit were packed and shipped in boxes the same as those used for oranges, and used labels identical in size, shape, and general advertising message.

AIRLINE
1940's
Fillmore

AIRSHIP
1940's*
Fillmore

AK-SAR-BEN
1920's**
Lemon Cove

AK-SAR-BEN
1940's
Lemon Cove

AK-SAR-BEN
1940's
Lemon Cove

ALBION
1920's*
Placentia

ALERT
1930's**
San Francisco

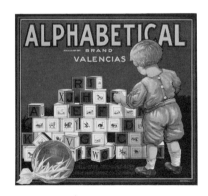

ALPHABETICAL
1930's***
Villa Park

ALTISSIMO
1920's
Placentia

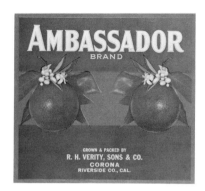

AMBASSADOR
1940's
Corona

ANACO
1920's*
San Francisco

ANA CO.
1920's*
San Francisco

ANDERSON'S
1930's
Lindsay

ANNIE LAURIE
1930's
Strathmore

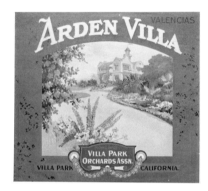

ARDEN VILLA
1920's***
Villa Park

ARROWHEAD
1930's*
East Highlands

ATHLETE
1930's
Claremont

ATLAS
1930's*
Olive

AVENUE
1920's
Riverside

BANANA BELT
1920's***
Villa Park

BARBARA WORTH
1920's**
Riverside

BARGAIN
1930's
Santa Paula

BARGAIN
1940's
Santa Paula

BARONY
1930's*
Anaheim

BELT
1930's
East Highlands

BIG BEN
1920's**
Orange

BIG J
1940's
San Francisco

BIRD ROCKS
1930's*
Villa Park

BLACK CRUSADER
1920's**
Azusa

BLACK HAWK
1920's**
Riverside

BLUE BANNER
1940's
Riverside

BLUE CIRCLE
1930's
Riverside

BLUE GOOSE
1940's
Los Angeles

BOB'S
1950's
Mecca

BONAFIDE
1920's*
Richgrove

BOULEVARD
1930's*
Claremont

BOUQUET
1920's*
Los Angeles

BOYHOOD
1920's**
Fontana

BRIDAL VEIL
1930's*
Santa Paula

BRONCO
1920's
Redlands

BROWNIES
1930's
Lemon Cove

BULL DOG
1920's*
Los Angeles

CAL-CREST
1940's
Riverside

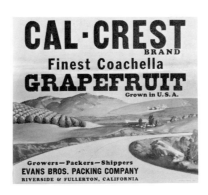

CAL-CREST
1940's
Riverside

CAL-EARLY
1940's
Riverside

CALEDONIA
1930's
Placentia

CAL-FLAVOR
1940's
Lindsay

CALIFORNIA DREAM
1920's*
Placentia

CALIFORNIA SUNSHINE
1930's*
Redlands

CAL-ORO
1920's***
Tustin

CAL-SWEET
1940's
Riverside

CAL-SWEET
1940's
Riverside

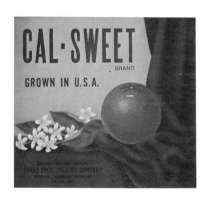

CAL-SWEET
1930's
Riverside

CALUMA
1940's
Corona

CAMBRIA
1930's
Placentia

CAMEL
1930's*
Corona

CAMELIA
1940's
Redlands

CARDINAL
1920's*
Orange

CAREFREE
1940's
Redlands

CARMEL
1930's**
East Highlands

CARRO AMANO
1920's
East Highlands

CASA BLANCA
1930's
Riverside

CASCADE O'GOLD
1940's
Exeter

CELESTE
1930's*
Olive

CERRITO
1940's
Highgrove

CHANTICLEER
1930's*
East Highlands

CHINESE
1920's***
Riverside

CITRUS COVE
1940's
Orange Cove

COCK OF THE WALK
1930's*
Orange

CO-ED
1940's
Claremont

COLLEGE HEIGHTS
1930's
Claremont

COLLEGIATE
1930's
Claremont

CONSUL
1940's
Corona

CORONA CROWN
1930's*
Corona

CORONA LILY
1930's
Corona

CRAFTON
1930's**
Mentone

CUPID
1920's*
Fillmore

CYCLE
1940's
Fillmore

DAHLIA
1940's
Redlands

DAISY
1930's
Covina

DASH
1940's
Santa Paula

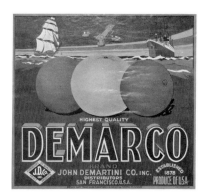

DEMARCO
1920's*
San Francisco

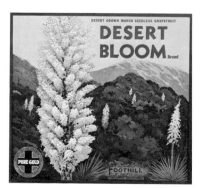

DESERT BLOOM
1930's*
Redlands

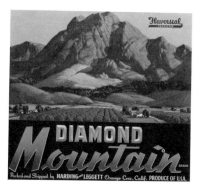

DIAMOND MOUNTAIN
1940's*
Orange Cove

DOMINANT
1940's
Porterville

DOMINANT
1930's*
Porterville

DOUBLE A
1930's
East Highlands

DR. FORBES
1940's
Coachella

DRAGON
1930's*
Redlands

DREAM FLOWER
1930's*
Orange

EAT-ONE
1930's
Lindsay

E.C.A.
1940's
Exeter

EL CAMINO
1920's*
Claremont

ENDURANCE
1930's*
Santa Paula

ENSIGN
1940's*

EPICURE
1930's
Orange

ESPERANZA
1940's
Placentia

ETIWANDA CREST
1930's
Etiwanda

EXCEPTIONAL
1940's
Santa Paula

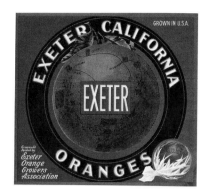

EXETER
1920's
Exeter

FANCIA
1920's*
Rialto

FARM BELLE
1940's*
Los Angeles

FEATURE
1940's*
Porterville

FIDELITY
1930's*
Glendora

FIDO
1930's* *
Orosi

FILLMORE CREST
1940's
Fillmore

FIRST CLASS
1930's*
Richgrove

FLAVOR
1940's
Corona

FLI-HI
1930's*
Tustin

FULL O'JUICE
1930's
Redlands

GETZBEST
1930's*
San Francisco

GILLETTE
1930's*
Lindsay

GLADIOLA
1920's
Covina

GLIDER
1930's*
Fillmore

GLOBES O'GOLD
1940's*
Orange Cove

GOLD BUCKLE
1930's
East Highlands

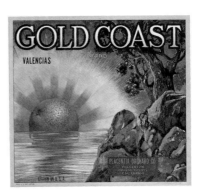

GOLD COAST
1930's*
Fullerton

GOLDEN CIRCLE
1930's
Redlands

GOLDEN EAGLE
1920's
Fullerton

GOLDEN GATE
1930's*
Lemon Cove

GOLDEN NEED
1930's*
Santa Paula

GOLDEN QUALITY
1930's*
Los Angeles

GOLDEN QUALITY
1930's*
Los Angeles

GOLDEN ROD
1930's
Redlands

GOLDEN SCEPTRE
1920's*
Rialto

GOLDEN TROUT
1930's*
Orange Cove

GOLDEN WEST
1920's**
Riverside

GONDOLIER
1930's
Fillmore

GOOD CHEER
1920's*
Porterville

GOOD CHEER
1940's
Porterville

GOODGIFT
1940's*
Ivanhoe

GOOD YEAR
1930's
Rayo

GRAND ENTRY
1940's
Orange Cove

GREAT VALLEY
1940's
Orange Cove

GREEN CIRCLE
1930's
Riverside

GREEN MILL
1920's*
Placentia

GREENSPOT
1920's
East Highlands

GREYHOUND
1920's*
North Pomona

HANDSUM
1930's
Strathmore

HAVE ONE
1930's
Lemon Cove

HEART OF CALIFORNIA
1930's
Exeter

HECTOR
1930's*
Olive

HIAWATHA
1930's*
Strathmore

HIGH BALL
1930's*
Exeter

HIGHLAND GROVE
1930's*
East Highlands

HIGHWAY
1920's**
Ontario

HILL BEAUTY
1940's
Porterville

HILL CHOICE
1940's
Porterville

HI-TONE
1930's
Upland

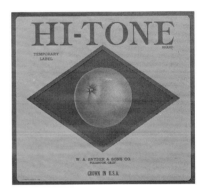

HI-TONE
1940's
Fullerton

HI-VALLEY
1930's*
Success

HOMER
1930's
Corona

HUMMING BIRD
1930's*
Santa Susana

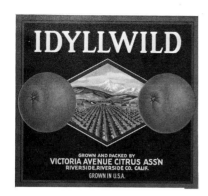

IDYLLWILD
1930's
Riverside

INDIAN BELLE
1915**
Porterville

INDIAN HILL
1915***
North Pomona

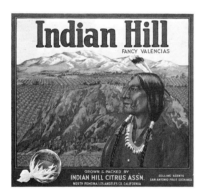

INDIAN HILL
1930's*
North Pomona

IRVALE
1940's
Irvine

JAMESON
1940's
Corona

JUCIFUL
1930's
Redlands

JUMBO
1930's*
San Francisco

JUSTRITE
1940's
Corona

KAWEAH RIVER BELLE
1930's*
Lemon Cove

KILTIE
1930's
Corona

KING DAVID
1930's
Placentia

KING'S PARK
1930's*
Ivanhoe

KOCHELA
1940's*
Thermal

LAGOON
1930's*
East Highlands

LA REINA
1920's
Rialto

LAUREL
1930's
Corona

LEGAL TENDER
1930's
Fillmore

LILY
1930's
Exeter

LINCOLN
1930's
Riverside

LINCOLN
1920's
Riverside

LINCOLN
1940's
Lincoln

LINEN
1930's
Irvine

LINWOOD
1940's
Corona

LOCHINVAR
1930's
East Highlands

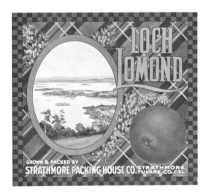

LOCH LOMOND
1930's
Strathmore

LOMA
1930's*
Santa Paula

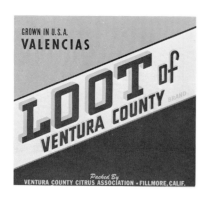

LOOT
1940's
Fillmore

MADRAS
1930's
Irvine

MAGNOLIA
1920's*
Porterville

MAHALA
1940's*
Highgrove

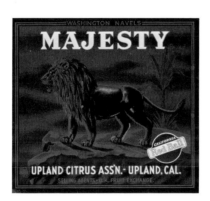

MAJESTY
1930's**
Upland

MAJORETTE
1930's
Woodlake

MAJORETTE
1920's**
Terra Bella

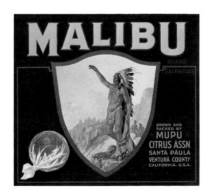

MALIBU
1920's*
Santa Paula

MALTA
1930's
Porterville

MANAGER
1930's*
Porterville

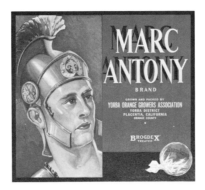

MARC ANTONY
1930's
Placentia

MARIPOSA
1930's*
Santa Paula

MARQUITA
1930's*
Arlington

MARVEL
1930's
Placentia

MASTER
1930's*
Porterville

MAZUMA
1920's***
Los Angeles

MEMORY
1920's*
Porterville

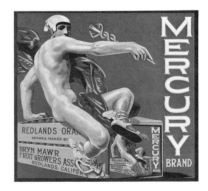

MERCURY
1920's***
Redlands

METROPOLITAN
1940's
Orange Cove

MINERAL KING
1920's*
Lemon Cove

MIRACLE
1920's
Placentia

MISSION BRIDGE
1920's***
Riverside

MOHAWK
1930's*
Orange

MONTE VISTA
1930's
Riverside

MOON
1920's
Greenspot

MORJON
1930's
San Francisco

MORNING GLORY
1920's*
North Pomona

MOUNTIE
1920's***
Villa Park

MUPU
1920's*
Santa Paula

MUSTANG
1930's*
Los Angeles

MUTT
1920's***
Porterville

NATIONAL
1930's*
Riverside

NATIVE DAUGHTER
1940's
Santa Paula

NAVAJO
1930's*
Riverside

NIMBLE
1940's
Santa Paula

OLD MISSION
1920's*
Fullerton

OLIVIA
1930's*
Olive

ORANGE CIRCLE
1940's
Orange Cove

ORANGE QUEEN
1920's***
Los Angeles

ORBIT
1930's*
Exeter

ORCHARD
1930's*
Riverside

ORCHARD KING
1930's
Covina

ORCHID
1920's*
Redlands

ORIOLE
1930's*
Fillmore

ORLAND
1930's
Orland

OROSI
1940's
Orosi

PACIFIC EXPORTER
1920's*
San Francisco

PACOAST
1930's
Los Angeles

PACOAST
1930's
Los Angeles

PALA BRAVE
1930's
Placentia

PANSY
1920's*
Redlands

PARAMOUNT
1930's*
Richgrove

PAR GOLD
1940's
Redlands

PATRICIAN
1920's**
Porterville

PAULA
1930's*
Santa Paula

PEP
1940's
Visalia

PINE CONE
1930's
East Highlands

PLANET
1930's*
Orange

PLEASANT
1930'**
Success

POCAHONTAS
1930's*
Strathmore

POINSETTIA
1930's*
Fillmore

POLO
1920's
East Highlands

POM-POM
1930's*
Sanger

PONCA
1930's
Porterville

PREFERRED
1930's
Covina

PREMIUM
1930's
Fullerton

PRESIDENT
1930's
Tustin

PRINCESS
1930's
Corona

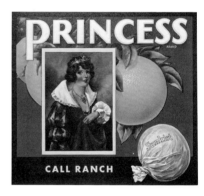

PRINCESS
1930's
Corona

PURE GOLD
1920's
Redlands

QUEEN ESTHER
1930's
Placentia

RAINBOW
1920's**
Lindsay

RAIN CROSS
1930's
Riverside

RAYO
1920's*
Rayo

REBECCA
1930's
Placentia

REBEL
1940's
Fillmore

RED BALL
1930's
Los Angeles

RED BIRD
1930's
Porterville

RED BOLERO
1940's
San Francisco

RED BOW
1930's*
Riverside

RED CAT
1930's***
Villa Park

RED CIRCLE
1930's
Riverside

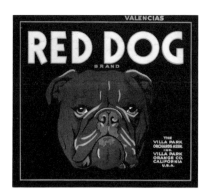

RED DOG
1930's***
Villa Park

RED MOUNTAIN
1930's
Corona

RED PEAK
1930's
Tustin

RED SKIN
1930's*
Rialto

REDSKIN
1920's*
Rialto

REDLANDS BEST
1930's
Redlands

REDLANDS CHOICE
1930's
Redlands

REDLANDS FOOTHILL
1930's
Redlands

REDLANDS JOY
1930's
Redlands

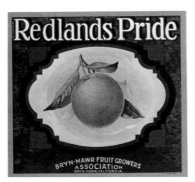

REDLANDS PRIDE
1930's
Redlands

REINDEER
1920's*
El Cajon

RISING SUN
1920's*

RIVERSIDE JEWEL
1940's
Riverside

RIVERSIDE SUPERFINE
1930's*
Riverside

ROCKY HILL
1930's
Exeter

ROOSTER
1930's*
Orange

ROSA DE ORO
1930's*
Thermalito

ROSE
1920's***
Redlands

ROYAL FEAST
1930's
Porterville

ROYAL KNIGHT
1930's
Redlands

RUBAIYAT
1930's
Redlands

RYAN & NEWTON CO.
1910***
Placentia

SAN ANTONIO
1930's
Ontario

SAN FRANCISCO
1930's**
San Francisco

SANTA
1930's**
Santa Paula

SATIN
1930's
Irvine

SCEPTER
1930's*
Orange

SCOTCH LASSIE JEAN
1930's
Strathmore

SEARCHLIGHT
1920's**
Orange

SEARCHLIGHT
1930's*
Orange

SEARCHLIGHT
1940's*
Orange

SELECTED
1930's*
Santa Paula

SENORITA
1940's
Santa Susana

SENTINEL BUTTE
1930's*
Woodlake

SERGE
1930's
Irvine

SHAMROCK
1930's
Placentia

SHAMROCK
1930's
Placentia

SHASTA
1920's*
Thermalito

SIERRA VISTA
1920's*
Porterville

SILVER BUCKLE
1930's
East Highlands

SILVER TIPS
1930's*
Tustin

SIMI
1930's*
Santa Susana

SKYROCKET
1940's
Exeter

S-L
1930's*
Porterville

SNOBOY
1940's
Los Angeles

SNYDER'S
1940's
Pomona

SOLID GOLD
1930's
Exeter

SOUTHLAND BEAUTIES
1940's
Corona

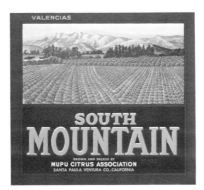

SOUTH MOUNTAIN
1930's
Santa Paula

SPLENDID
1920's*
Ivanhoe

SPRAY
1930's
Etiwanda

SQUIRREL
1920's*
Riverside

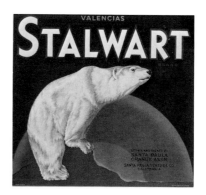

STALWART
1930's*
Santa Paula

STANDARD
1930's*
Riverside

STAR
1920's
Sunshine

STAR DUST
1930's*
Exeter

STAR OF CALIFORNIA
1930's
Exeter

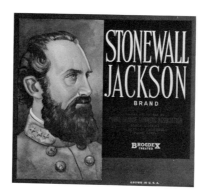

STONEWALL JACKSON
1930's*
Placentia

STORK
1930's*
Claremont

STRATHMORE
1930's
Strathmore

STRENGTH
1930's*
Santa Paula

SUBURBAN
1920's**
Lindsay

SUMCLASS
1940's*
Los Angeles

SUMMIT
1930's
Redlands

SUN
1920's
East Highlands

SUNFLOWER
1920's
Redlands

SUN GARDEN
1930's*
Porterville

SUN IDOL
1940's
Ivanhoe

SUNKIST
1930's
Los Angeles

SUNKIST
1930's
Los Angeles

SUNLAND STANDARDS
1930's*
Porterville

SUNNY COVE
1920's
Redlands

SUNNY HEIGHTS
1930's
Redlands

SUN PRINCE
1930's
Orange Cove

SUN-TAG
1940's
Placentia

SUPERFINE
1930's
Riverside

SURPASS
1940's
Exeter

SWEETREAT
1920's*
Orange

SYMBOL
1930's
Riverside

TA-CHE
1930's*
Santa Paula

TALISMAN
1930's
Redlands

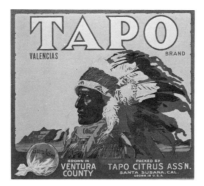

TAPO
1930's*
Santa Susana

TARTAN
1930's
Corona

TEA
1930's
Lindsay

TESORO RANCHO
1930's
Placentia

THREE ARCHES
1930's*
Villa Park

365
1940's
Upland

TICK-TOCK
1930's**
Villa Park

TOM CAT
1930's**
Orosi

TOM'S BEST
1940's

TRADE-WIN
1940's*
Los Angeles

TREE TOP
1940's
Lemon Cove

TROJAN
1930's*
Olive

TROPIX
1940's*
Woodlake

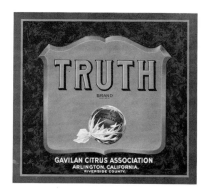

TRUTH
1930's
Riverside

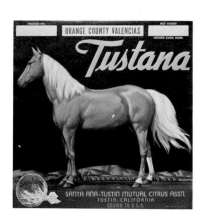

TUSTANA
1930's*
Tustin

TWEED
1930's
Irvine

TWIN TREE
1940's
Lemon Cove

UNABEST
1920's*
Woodlake

UNAFINE
1920's*
Woodlake

UNAGOOD
1920's*
Woodlake

UNICORN
1930's*
East Highlands

UPLAND PRIDE
1930's
Upland

VALLEY VIEW
1930's
Claremont

VALUE
1940's**
Porterville

VANDALIA
1920's***
Plano

VANDALIA
1930's
Porterville

VELVET
1930's
Irvine

VENICE COVE
1930's
Ivanhoe

VICTOR
1930's*
Etiwanda

VICTORIA
1930's
Riverside

VICTORIA
1930's
Riverside

VIGOR
1930's**
San Francisco

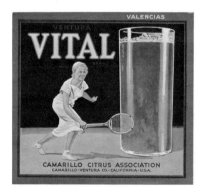

VITAL
1930's**
Camarillo

VOLUNTEER
1920's*
North Pomona

WARRIOR
1930's*
North Pomona

WASHINGTON
1930's
Exeter

WESTERN QUEEN
1920's*
Rialto

WESTERN QUEEN
1930's*
Rialto

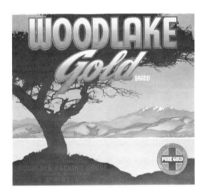

WOODLAKE GOLD
1930's
Woodlake

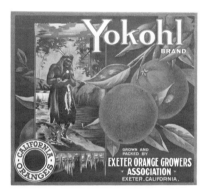

YOKOHL
1920's
Exeter

YO-SEMI-TE
1920's*
Ivanhoe

YUCCA
1920's
Redlands

YUMA CHIEF
1930's**
Redlands

ZEUS
1930's*
Olive

LEMONS

Successful lemon growing requires a cool climate without freezing temperatures, with relative freedom from strong winds. These conditions exist near the ocean in Ventura and Santa Barbara counties north of Los Angeles, in localized areas in San Bernardino and Riverside counties, and in the central California valley foothills.

The industry began to develop in the late 1890's, and since 1920 has been about a quarter as large as the California orange industry. In contrast to oranges and grapefruit—which are grown in Arizona, Texas, and Florida as well as in California—all commercial lemon crops in the United Sates are grown in California.

Lemons are shipped in a flatter box than oranges, with a label about 11″ x 9″. Consumers usually buy lemons in smaller quantities than oranges, and buy them on a seasonal basis. This led to a need for an advertising message on lemon labels promoting the fruit's refreshing and healthful qualities. Many labels featured seaside orchards, brisk ocean scenes, and the use of lemons in lemonade and pies.

Lemons and oranges sometimes were sold by the same shipper, using the same basic design for both labels, changing it only slightly to take the different label dimensions into account.

The use of lemon labels ended at the same time as orange labels, in the mid 1950's.

A-1
1930's
Los Angeles

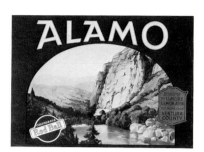

ALAMO
1930's*
Fillmore

ALBION
1930's
Placentia

ALISO
1930's
Carpinteria

ALL YEAR
1930's
Fillmore

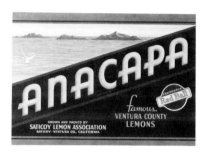

ANACAPA
1930's
Saticoy

AQUA
1930's
Ventura

ARAB
1930's*
San Dimas

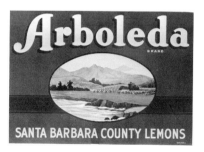

ARBOLEDA
1930's
Goleta

ATHLETE
1930's
Claremont

BASKET
1930's
Lemon Cove

BASKETBALL
1920's*
Claremont

BESGRADE
1940's
Oxnard

BLUE STAR
1930's*
Los Angeles

BRIDAL VEIL
1930's*
Santa Paula

BULL DOG
1920's*
Los Angeles

BY THE SEA
1930's
Montalvo

CAL-CREST
1940's
Riverside

CAMBRIA
1930's
Placentia

CAMPUS
1930's*
Claremont

CHANNEL
1930's
Goleta

CO-ED
1940's
Claremont

COLLEGE HEIGHTS
1930's
Claremont

COLLEGIATE
1930's
Claremont

COLLIE
1920's*
San Dimas

COMET
1930's*
Villa Park

COMPASS
1930's*
Santa Paula

CORONA BEAUTY
1940's
Corona

COY
1940's
Saticoy

CUB
1930's
Upland

CUSTOM
1940's
Santa Paula

CUTTER
1940's
Oxnard

DEL NORTE
1940's
Oxnard

DIPLOMAT
1930's
Corona

DOMESTIC
1930's*
Corona

DUCK
1920's*
San Dimas

EL MERITO
1940's
Santa Paula

EL PRIMO
1930's*
Claremont

ENCORE
1940's
Porterville

ENVOY
1930's
Corona

ESTERO
1930's
Goleta

EVENING STAR
1930's
San Fernando

EVERGREEN
1930's*
Villa Park

EXCELLENT
1940's
Santa Paula

EXCLUSIVE
1930's
Ivanhoe

EXPOSITION
1920's
Santa Barbara

FALLBROOK
1930's
Fallbrook

FESTIVAL
1920's
Santa Barbara

FIDO
1930's*
Orosi

FIRST AMERICAN
1920's**
Los Angeles

FONTANA GIRL
1918**
Fontana

FOUNTAIN
1920's***
Santa Paula

FULL WORTH
1930's*
Santa Paula

GALLEON
1920's
Oxnard

GATEWAY
1930's
Lemon Cove

GOLDEN BOWL
1920's*
Santa Paula

GOLDEN ROD
1930's
Des Moines

GOLDEN STATE
1930's
Lemon Cove

GOLDEN V
1940's*
Ventura

GOLETA
1930's
Goleta

GREYHOUND
1930's*
San Dimas

GUIDE
1940's
Saticoy

HARDY
1940's
Santa Paula

HARMONY
1920's*
San Dimas

HARVEST
1940's
Santa Barbara

HELENA
1930's
Ventura

HERMOSA
1930's
Fallbrook

HONEYMOON
1920's*
Los Angeles

HOUSEHOLD
1940's
Porterville

INDEX
1920's*
La Habra

INDEX SUPREME
1930's
La Habra

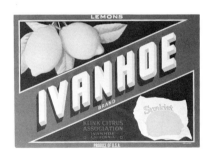

IVANHOE
1940's
Ivanhoe

JUST AS GOOD
1930's
Lemon Cove

JUSTRITE
1940's
Corona

KAWEAH MAID
1920's
Lemon Cove

KEEPER
1940's
Santa Paula

KILTIE
1930's
Corona

KING TUT
1920's
Santa Barbara

LA PATERA
1930's
Goleta

LAS FUENTES
1920's*
Montecito

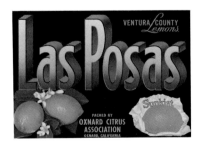

LAS POSAS
1930's
Oxnard

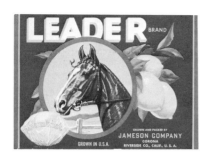

LEADER
1930's
Corona

LEGAL-PAK
1940's*
Riverside

LEMONADE
1930's
Ivanhoe

LEVEL
1930's*
Santa Paula

LINWOOD
1940's
Corona

LOFTY
1930's
Fallbrook

MADURO
1940's
Corona

MARINER
1930's
Carpinteria

MARVEL
1930's
Placentia

MAVERICK
1930's*
Corona

METEOR
1930's
San Fernando

MINERVA
1930's
Corona

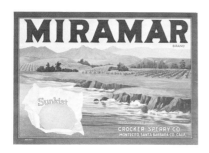

MIRAMAR
1930's*
Montecito

MISSION
1930's*
Santa Barbara

MONTALVO
1930's*
Saticoy

MONTECITO VALLEY
1920's*
Montecito

MORNING CHEER
1940's
Porterville

MORNING SMILE
1940's
Porterville

MORNING SUN
1930's
San Fernando

OCEAN SPRAY
1920's*
Santa Paula

OCEAN VIEW
1930's
Carpinteria

OH-CEE
1930's
Orange Cove

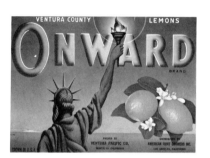

ONWARD
1930's*
Montalvo

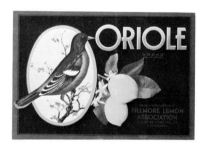

ORIOLE
1930's*
Fillmore

OXNARD
1930's
Oxnard

PACIFIC
1930's
Santa Barbara

PACIFIC MAID
1930's*
Montalvo

PANAMA
1930's
Santa Barbara

PANSY
1930's*
Redlands

PARADE
1930's
Saticoy

PASSPORT
1940's
Corona

PAULA
1930's*
Santa Paula

PAUL NEYRON
1930's*
La Verne

PERFECTION
1930's
Ivanhoe

PERFECTION
1940's
Ivanhoe

PET
1920's*
San Dimas

PITCHER
1930's*
Santa Paula

POPPY
1930's*
Redlands

POWER
1930's
Ventura

PRIDE OF CORONA
1940's
Corona

PRIDE OF CORONA
1930's
Corona

PROGRESSIVE
1940's
Corona

PUP
1920's*
San Dimas

RADIANT
1920's*
Villa Park

RAMONA
1920's
San Fernando

RED BALL
1930's
Los Angeles

RED FAN
1930's*
Orange Cove

REGENT
1940's
Santa Paula

ROUGH DIAMOND
1930's
Santa Paula

SAN ANTONIO
1930's
Ontario

SAN MARCOS
1930's
Goleta

SANTA
1930's
Santa Paula

SANTA BARBARA
1930's*
Santa Barbara

SANTA MARGUERITA
1920's
Fallbrook

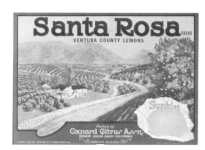

SANTA ROSA
1920's*
Oxnard

SANTA ROSA
1930's
Oxnard

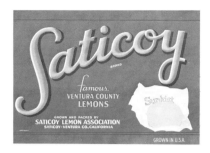

SATICOY
1940's
Saticoy

SCHOONER
1930's
Goleta

SEA BIRD
1930's
Carpinteria

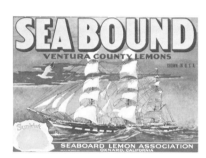

SEA BOUND
1930's
Oxnard

SEA BREEZE
1930's
Carpinteria

SEA COAST
1930';s
Ventura

SEA COOL
1940's
Oxnard

SEA CURED
1930's
Oxnard

SEA GROVES
1940's
Oxnard

SEA GULL
1930's
Upland

SEA LIGHT
1940's
Carpinteria

SEASIDE
1930's
Oxnard

SEATREAT
1930's*
Carpinteria

SELVA
1930's
Fillmore

SELECTED
1930's
Santa Paula

SENATOR
1930's
Tustin

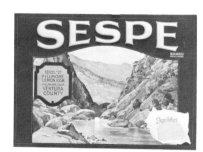

SESPE
1930's
Fillmore

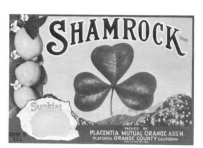

SHAMROCK
1930's
Placentia

SILVER CORD
1930's
Santa Paula

SILVER MOON
1930's
San Fernando

SOLO
1930's
Saticoy

SOMISEA
1940's
Oxnard

SOUTHERN CROSS
1930's**
San Fernando

SOUTHLAND BEAUTIES
1940's
Corona

SPARKLE
1930's
Saticoy

SPLENDID
1930's
Ivanhoe

SPRAY
1940's
Etiwanda

STRAND
1930's
Oxnard

SUMMERLAND
1930's*
Montecito

SUNFLOWER
1920's
Des Moines

SUNKIST
1930's
Los Angeles

SUNSET
1930's
Corona

SUNSIDE
1940's
Santa Paula

SUPERBA
1940's
Santa Paula

SUPERFINE
1930's
Riverside

TARTAN
1930's
Corona

TEPIC
1940's
Saticoy

TERRIER
1920's*
Los Angeles

THREE STAR
1930's**
East Whittier

TOM CAT
1930's*
Orosi

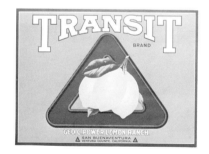

TRANSIT
1920's
Ventura

TREE-O
1940's
La Habra

UMPIRE
1920's**
Claremont

UNAGOOD
1920's*
Woodlake

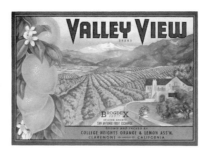

VALLEY VIEW
1930's
Claremont

VENTURA MAID
1930's*
Montalvo

VESPER
1930's
Porteville

WAVE
1940's
Santa Paula

WHITE CROSS
1930's
Santa Paula

WHIZ
1930's
Saticoy

WILDFLOWER
1920's*
Los Angeles

CALIFORNIA APPLES

While apples have been grown in nearly all parts of California, major commercial production is centered in two relatively small areas, the Pajaro Valley near Watsonville, about 80 miles south of San Francisco, and the Sebastopol area near the Russian River, about 60 miles north of San Francisco.

The Pajaro Valley industry was developed in the 1890's by immigrants from the area now known as Yugoslavia, who continue to be the main growers and marketers of Watsonville fruit. Due to the prevalence of fog and the lack of sharp frosty nights prior to harvest, red varieties of apples do not attain a high color in this region. The most successful commercial variety is the yellow Newtown Pippin, a hard, crisp, juicy apple which ripens in the late fall.

Apple production started in the Sebastopol area in the early 1900's. The main variety grown is the Gravenstein, a red striped apple which ripens in the summer, before fruit from most other areas is ready for market.

Since California apples were shipped by rail, the bushel basket and the barrel used in the East were not satisfactory. A rectangular box with a volume of approximately a bushel was developed. A label about 10¼ " x 9" was customarily used. Apples were shipped directly from the Watsonville and Sebastopol areas, as well as by large distributors in San Francisco.

Apple labels on wooden boxes were used somewhat later than citrus labels, with a gradual transition taking place in the late 1950's and early 1960's.

AIRSHIP
1920's**
Watsonville

APPLES
1920's
Visalia

APPLES
1920's

APPLETON
1915
Watsonville

BACHAN
1930's
Watsonville

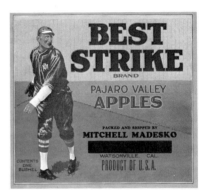

BEST STRIKE
1920's*
Watsonville

B GRADE
1900*
Watsonville

BIRD VALLEY
1920's
Watsonville

BITE SIZE
1940's
Watsonville

BLUE FLAG
1920's
Watsonville

BOA-VISTA
1940's
Placerville

BOLERO
1940's
San Francisco

BUFFALO
1930's
Watsonville

BUTTERFLY
1930's
Watsonville

CAMEL
1900*
Watsonville

DIVING GIRL
1920's
Watsonville

DOUBLE FEATURE
1940's
Watsonville

EN AVANT
1920's*
San Francisco

F.B.
1915*
Watsonville

FLAG
1920's
Watsonville

GILT EDGE
1918*
Watsonville

GOLDEN WEST
1910*
Watsonville

GREEN
1920's
Watsonville

JACKIE BOY
1930's
Sebastopol

J.M.L.
1900***
Watsonville

J.M.L.
1920's*
Watsonville

LAKE VIEW
1910
Watsonville

LAKE VIEW
1930's
Watsonville

LARSEN
1950's
Placerville

LEGAL TENDER
1920's*
Watsonville

LGB
1915*
Watsonville

LUCKY STRIKE
1920's
Watsonville

LUCKY TRAIL
1915*
Watsonville

L-Z
1940's
San Francisco

MADESKO
1940's
Watsonville

MORJON
1930's
San Francisco

MORJON
1930's
San Francisco

MORJON
1930's
San Francisco

MORNING STAR
1920's*
Watsonville

MORNING STAR
1930's
Watsonville

MT. MADONNA
1940's
Watsonville

NIGHTINGALE
1920's*
Watsonville

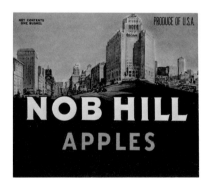

NOB HILL
1940's*
San Francisco

N S P
1930's
Watsonville

PACIFIC PRIDE
1940's
San Francisco

PANAMA PACIFIC
1915***
Watsonville

PARADISE
1950's
Paradise

PEACOCK
1900**
Watsonville

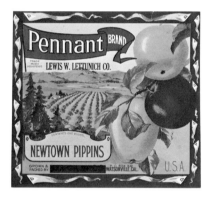

PENNANT
1915*
Watsonville

PINE CREST
1930's*
Pine Crest

PIONEER
1930's
Sacramento

PREMIUM
1940's
Watsonville

PRIDE
1915*
Watsonville

RED DIAMOND
1920's
Watsonville

RED HEART
1915*
Watsonville

RED STAR
1920's
Watsonville

ROSE HILL
1910**
Watsonville

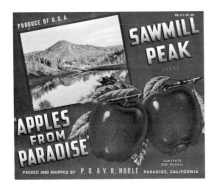

SAWMILL PEAK
1940's
Paradise

SEBASTOPOL QUALITY
1950's
Graton

SEBASTOPOL QUEEN
1950's
Graton

SENORITA
1930's
San Francisco

SIERRA GLEN
1950's
Sonora

SNOW-LINE
1930's
Oakglen

SOLO
1910***
Watsonville

STAR-PAK
1940's*
Watsonville

SUN FLAVOR
1940's
Watsonville

SUNKIST
1915*
Watsonville

SUNKIST
1950's
Watsonville

TIGER
1920's*
Watsonville

TOP PEAK
1940's
Redlands

TOP PEAK
1930's
Redlands

UTILITY
1920's*
Watsonville

VALLEY
1950's
Watsonville

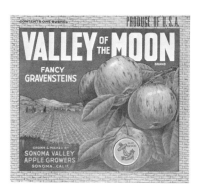

VALLEY OF THE MOON
1930's*
Sonoma

WATSONVILLE
1920's*
Watsonville

WHITE STAR
1920's*
Watsonville

WILKO
1940's
San Francisco

WILKO
1940's
San Francisco

WILKO
1940's
San Francisco

WINGED WHEEL
1940's
San Francisco

WASHINGTON APPLES

The main apple growing areas in the United States are in the Yakima and Wenachee valleys in central Washington, east of the Cascade Mountains. The climate, with sunny weather and cool nights, is ideal for apples. The industry, which developed in the early 1900's when irrigation water became available, has always been large and fragmented, with hundreds of growers and shippers. Many varieties of apples are grown, with the Delicious, Winesap, Jonathan, Rome Beauty, and Yellow Newtown being of primary commercial importance.

Wooden boxes with the same dimensions as those used in California were used for Washington apples. The box labels were the same size and format. A design theme that appears on many labels shows the streams, lakes, and waterfalls of the Cascade foothills. As in California, the wooden boxes were gradually replaced with cardboard boxes in the late 1950's and early 1960's.

Thousands of Washington apple labels were designed and used, but have not been studied and categorized as well as the California citrus labels. The labels shown here should be taken as representative samples, rather than a complete listing of all labels available at reasonable prices.

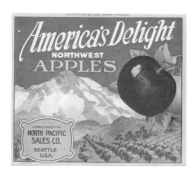

AMERICA'S DELIGHT
1920's
Seattle

ANACO
1940's
Hood River

ANCHOR
1920's*
Yakima

APPLE KIDS
1940's
Cowiche

BABY
1920's
Seattle

BEST BOX
1920's*
Yakima

BLEWETT PASS
1940's
Cashmere

BLUE RIBBON
1930's
Yakima

BLUE SEAL
1920's
Wenatchee

BLUE WINNER
1940's
Okanogan

BLUE Z
1920's
Yakima

BUCKAROO
1930's*
Wenatchee

BUTLER'S PRIDE
1950's
Wenatchee

CHERE BEST
1940's
Wenatchee

CHIEF JOSEPH
1940's
Yakima

CHOICE OF CHELAN
1930's
Wenatchee

CLASEN
1940's
Yakima

CLASS "A"
1950's
Yakima

CLIFF
1930's
Chelan

CLIPPER SHIP
1920's*
Wenatchee

COLOR GUARD
1940's
Wenatchee

COLUMBIA BELLE
1940's
Wenatchee

CONGDON
1940's
Yakima

CRYSTAL PEAK
1940's
Yakima

DAINTY MAID
1940's
Wenatchee

DEEP BLUE SEA
1920's
Wapato

DEPEND-ON
1930's
Yakima

DON'T WORRY
1940's
Yakima

DYNAMO
1930's
Wenatchee

EATUM
1950's
Yakima

EATUM-RITE
1940's
Hood River

ELITE
1940's
Wenatchee

EMERALD GREEN
1930's
Yakima

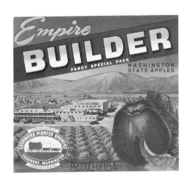

EMPIRE BUILDER
1940's
Cashmere

ENPEE
1930's
Seattle

ENSIGN
1920's*
Portland

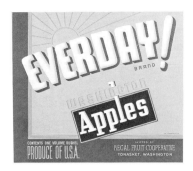

EVERDAY!
1940's
Tonasket

FALLS
1930's
Chelan

FASHION PLATE
1940's
Wenatchee

FOUR STAR
1940's
Cashmere

FRIGID-APS
1940's
Yakima

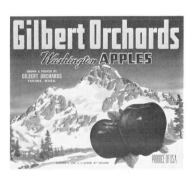

GILBERT ORCHARDS
1940's
Yakima

GLACIER PEAK
1940's*
Wenatchee

GOLDEN RING
1920's
Yakima

GOLDEN SPUR
1940's
Yakima

GOODFRUIT
1930's
Yakima

GOOD PICKENS
1940's
Cashmere

GOSLING
1930's*
Hood River

GOVERNOR WINTHROP
1930's*
Yakima

GRAND COULEE
1930's
Coulee

GREAT-NORTHWEST
1930's
Wenatchee

HAMILTON'S
1940's
Wenatchee

HAPPY APPLE
1940's
Yakima

HARVEST TIME
1930's
Yakima

HEADLINE
1940's
Wenatchee

HEART OF WASHINGTON
1950's
Malaga

HEAVYPACK
1930's
Oroville

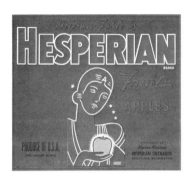

HESPERIAN
1930's
Wenatchee

HI BUV ALL
1940's
Wenatchee

HI SEA
1930's
Wenatchee

HI-YU
1930's
Wenatchee

HULA
1930's
Seattle

HUNTER
1930's
Wenatchee

HY-LAND KIDS
1940's
Cowiche

HY-TONE
1930's
Wenatchee

HY-VALLEY
1940's
Yakima

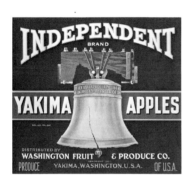

INDEPENDENT
1920's
Yakima

INDEPENDENT
1920's
Yakima

JACK'S
1940's
Cashmere

JIM HILL
1940's
Wenatchee

JIM WADE
1930's
Wenatchee

JO-JO
1930's
Wenatchee

JOLLY JIM
1930's*
Chelan

KARE-FUL-PAK
1930's
Yakima

KILE
1940's
Yakima

KYTE
1920's
Yakima

LAKE CHELAN
1940's
Chelan

LAKE WENATCHEE
1930's
Cashmere

LAMB
1940's
Yakima

LAURIE
1940's

LOOP LOOP
1930's*
Malott

LUCKY LAD
1920's*
Yakima

LURE
1930's*
Oroville

MAD RIVER
1940's
Entiat

MISCHIEF
1950's
Wenatchee

MOUNTAIN
1930's
Portland

MOUNTAIN GOAT
1930's
Chelan

MT. HOOD
1920's
Hood River

MR. APPLE
1950's
Yakima

NEW DEAL
1930's

NUCHIEF
1940's
Wenatchee

NUCHIEF
1950's
Wenatchee

NUCHIEF
1940's
Wenatchee

O-FINE-O
1940's
Wenatchee

ORCHARD BOY
1940's
Selah

OUR PRIDE
1920's*

OX TEAM
1930's
Wenatchee

PELICAN
1920's
Yakima

PETER PAN
1930's
Wenatchee

PETE'S BEST
1950's
Yakima

PIC-O-PETE
1920's
Yakima

PLEN TEE COLOR
1940's
Yakima

RAINIER
1930's*
Yakima

REDMAN
1930's
Wenatchee

RED WAGON
1940's
Yakima

RED WINNER
1940's
Okanogan

REGAL RED
1930's
Yakima

REPETITION
1930's
Yakima

RODEO
1940's*
Wenatchee

ROSE
1940's
Wenatchee

SAILS
1920's
Wenatchee

SCARLET SPICE
1950's
Wenatchee

SHEARER
1930's
Tieton

SKOOKUM
1940's
Chelan

SKOOKUM
1920's*
Mallot

SKOOKUM
1920's*
Omak

SKY RANCH
1940's
Yakima

SNOW OWL
1920's
Yakima

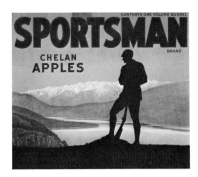

SPORTSMAN
1930's*
Chelan

STATE SEAL
1920's
Seattle

STRAND'S
1930's
Cowiche

SURETY
1920's*
Yakima

SWAN
1920's
Yakima

SWEET SUE
1930's
Wenatchee

TEACHER'S PET
1950's*
Manson

TENNIS
1930's
Seattle

TIE-IT-ON
1930's*
Tieton

TOPAZ
1930's
Wenatchee

TOP BOX
1940's
Yakima

TRITON
1930's
Yakima

TROJAN
1930's
Wenatchee

TROUT
1940's
Chelan

TULIP
1920's
Yakima

TUMWATER
1940's
Cashmere

TWIN W
1920's
Wenatchee

U-LIKE-UM
1930's*
Cashmere

UNCLE SAM
1920's
Wapato

VIOLET
1920's
Yakima

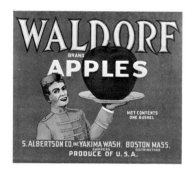

WALDORF
1930's
Yakima

WENOKA
1930's
Wenatchee

WESTERN
1930's*
Yakima

WESTERN STAR
1920's*
Yakima

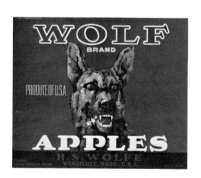

WOLF
1920's
Wenatchee

YAKIMA CHIEF
1930's
Yakima

YAKIMA VALLEY
1920's
Wapato

YUM-YUM
1930's*
Wenatchee

STOCK LABEL
1930's

STOCK LABEL
1920's

STOCK LABEL
1930's

STOCK LABEL
1940's

PEARS

Pears are grown commercially in scattered areas of north central California, and in Oregon and Washington. In California, the main areas are the rich, moist lands of the Sacramento River delta, the cooler foothills of the Sacramento and San Joaquin River valleys, and in Santa Clara County. In Oregon, pears are grown in the Hood River area, east of Portland near the Columbia River. In Washington, the main area is in the Wenachee and Yakima valleys, the same general area where apples are grown. The industry in these three states, which developed in the 1920's, is now the most highly commercialized pear growing region in the world.

The principal variety grown in California is the Bartlett; additional varieties grown in Oregon and Washington include the Bosc and d'Anjou.

Pears were packed in rectangular wooden boxes containing 4/5 bushel, somewhat smaller than apple boxes. The label size was somewhat variable, usually about 10½" x 7½".

As with other wooden fruit boxes, pear boxes gradually were replaced by cardboard boxes in the late 1950's.

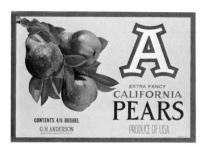

A
1940's
San Juan Bautista

ALL GOOD
1940's
Yakima

AMERICAN MAID
1940's
Los Angeles

A PLUS
1930's
Entiat

AUBURN
1940's
Auburn

BEAR CREEK
1930's*
Medford

BEE-N
1950's
San Jose

BELLBOY
1930's
Seattle

BIG CITY
1930's
Suisun

BIG GAME
1930's
Walnut Grove

BLAZING STAR
1940's
Kelseyville

BLUE ANCHOR
1940's
Sacramento

BLUE BIRD
1940's
Peshastin

BLUE CIRCLE
1940's
Suisun

BLUE FLAG
1950's
San Francisco

BLUE GOOSE
1940's
Lodi

BLUE MOUNTAIN
1940's
Walla Walla

BLUE PARROT
1930's*
San Francisco

BLUE Z
1930's
Yakima

BOY BLUE
1940's
Wenatchee

BUCKINGHAM
1920's
Vacaville

BUTTE
1930's
Hamilton City

B-WISE
1930's*
Sacramento

CAL-CHIEF
1920's*
Suisun

CALIFORNIA BEAUTY
1930's
Fresno

CALIFORNIA MOUNTAIN
1920's*
Penryn

CAL-JUNIOR
1920's*
Suisun

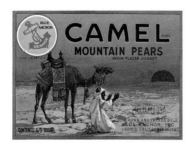

CAMEL
1930's
Loomis

CAPITAL PAK
1940's
Sacramento

CASCADIAN
1940's
Wenatchee

CHEKOLA
1915*
North Yakima

COCK-I-TOO
1930's*
Sacramento

COLFAX
1940's
Colfax

COVERED WAGON
1930's
Newcastle

DANIELSON'S
1920's*
Suisun

DEL RIO
1940's
Medford

DIAMOND S
1940's*
Hood

DI GIORGIO
1950's
San Francisco

DON JUAN
1940's
San Juan Bautista

DONNER
1930's
Auburn

DON'T WORRY
1940's
Yakima

DOUBLE EAGLE
1920's
San Jose

DUCKWALL
1930's
Hood River

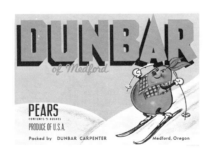

DUNBAR
1950's
Medford

EAGLE
1950's
Santa Clara

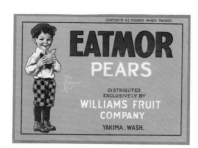

EATMOR
1920's*
Yakima

EATUM
1930's
Yakima

EATUM-RIPE
1940's
Hood River

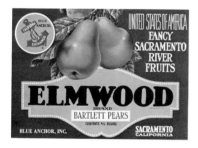

ELMWOOD
1940's
Sacramento

EL RIO ORCHARD
1950's
San Francisco

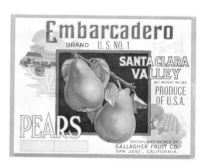

EMBARCADERO
1920's
San Jose

EMERALD BEAUTY
1930's*
Wenatchee

ESKIMO
1920's**
Medford

FAR WEST
1920's
Seattle

FASHION PLATE
1940's
Wenatchee

FEDERATED
1930's
San Francisco

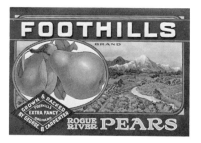

FOOTHILLS
1920's*
Medford

FOREVER FIRST
1950's
Sacramento

401
1940's
Medford

FOUR STAR
1940's
Wenatchee

FREITAS
1940's
San Juan Bautista

FRUIT BOWL
1940's
Selah

GEM
1950's
Sacramento

GOLD CIRCLE
1940's
Suisun

GOLD CREST
1940's
Marysville

GOLDEN
1930's
Medford

GOLDEN BOSC
1930's
Medford

GOLDEN RANGE
1950's
Suisun

GOLDEN ROD
1930's
Yakima

GOVERNOR WINTHROP
1930's*
Yakima

GRAND COULEE
1940's
Coulee

GRAND PRIZE
1915*
Chicago Park

H
1940's
San Juan Bautista

HAMILTON'S
1930's
Wenatchee

HARVEST MOON
1930's
Yakima

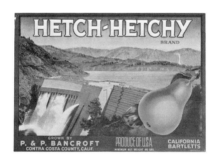

HETCH-HETCHY
1930's
Contra Costa

HIGHCROFT
1940's
Medford

HIGH-HAND
1930's
Loomis

HUSTLER
1920's
Courtland

ILLIHEE
1940's
Medford

INDEPENDENT
1930's
Yakima

JIM WADE
1930's
Wenatchee

KEYSTONE
1930's
Entiat

LADY OF THE LAKE
1940's
Kelseyville

LAKE COUNTY DIAMOND
1930's
Finley

LAKE COUNTY PREMIUM
1930's
Ukiah

LAKECOVE
1930's*
Finley

LAKE GOLD
1940's
Sacramento

LAKE RIDGE
1930's
Kelseyville

LAKE WENATCHEE
1940's
Cashmere

LIFE
1930's
Walnut Grove

L.L.
1920's*
Suisun

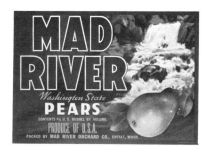

MAD RIVER
1940's
Entiat

MAGIC LAKE
1930's*
Sacramento

MAJESTIC
1930's
Yakima

MAJORPAK
1930's*
Tacoma

MALTESE CROSS
1930's
Medford

MARYKA
1950's
Kelseyville

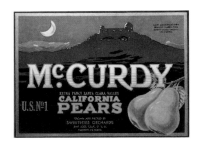

McCURDY
1920's
San Jose

MENDOCINO
1940's
Sacramento

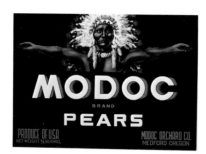

MODOC
1940's
Medford

MOPAC
1940's
Medford

MORJON
1940's
Seattle

MOTHER'S
1930's*

MOUNTAIN EDGE
1950's
Yakima

MT. HOOD
1920's*
Hood River

MT. KONOCTI
1930's
Kelseyville

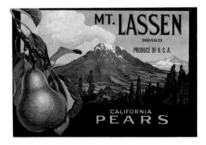

MT. LASSEN
1930's
Hamilton City

MT. PITT
1940's
Medford

MT. SHASTA
1930's
Hamilton City

NOB HILL
1940's
San Francisco

OH YES!
1950's
San Francisco

OLD GOLD
1930's
Medford

OLD ORCHARD
1920's
Santa Clara

ONEONTA
1940's
Wenatchee

ORCHARD
1920's*
YAKIMA

OREGON ORCHARDS
1940's
Medford

OUR PICK
1930's*
Loomis

OUT OF THE WEST
1930's
Santa Clara

PALO ALTO
1930's
Santa Clara

PARADISE
1920's
Suisun

PANORAMA
1930's
Hood River

PEACOCK
1930's
Sacramento

PEACOCK
1950's
Sacramento

PIC O PAC
1940's
Medford

PIGGY
1940's
Medford

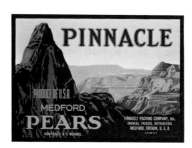

PINNACLE
1930's
Medford

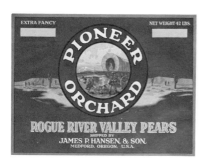

PIONEER
1920's*
Medford

PIONEER
1940's
Sacramento

PIRATE'S COVE
1930's
Finley

PLACER
1930's*
Auburn

PLACERVILLE DARTLAND
1950's
Placerville

PLACERVILLE PONY EXPRESS
1940's*
Placerville

PLACERVILLE TAHOE
1930's
Placerville

PLACERVILLE TAHOE
1940's
Placerville

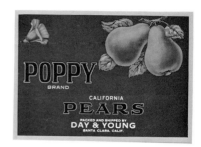

POPPY
1950's
Santa Clara

PRIDE OF THE RIVER
1920's*
Locke

QUAIL
1930's*
Sacramento

QUERCUS RANCH
1930's
Kelseyville

RANCHERIA
1930's
Suisun

RED CIRCLE
1940's
Suisun

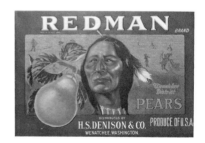

REDMAN
1930's*
Wenatchee

RED MOON
1930's*
Ukiah

RIVER BOY
1930's
Sacramento

RIVER MAID
1930's
Fullerton

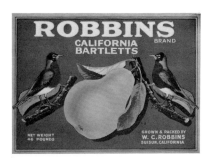

ROBBINS
1920's*
Suisun

ROSE
1940's
Wenatchee

ROSE GOLD
1930's
Yuba City

ROUND ROBIN
1930's
Medford

SANCLAR
1940's
San Jose

SCOTTY
1940's
Walnut Grove

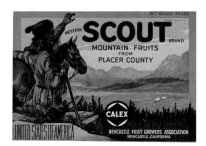

SCOUT
1930's**
New Castle

SMILING THRU
1930's
Sacramento

SNOW CREST
1940's
Marysville

SNOW OWL
1920's
Yakima

SPAN
1930's*
Walnut Grove

STAGECOACH
1930's
Medford

STAR POINT
1940's
Kelseyville

STATUE
1940's
Suisun

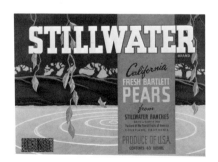

STILLWATER
1940's
Courtland

SUMMIT
1930's
Colfax

SUNDAY BEST
1950's
Medford

SUNGIFT
1920's
Wenatchee

SUNSHINE RANCH
1930's
Wapato

SUN SMILE
1930's
Colfax

SUN SUGARED
1950's
Medford

SWAN
1920's
Yakima

T-HACHA-P
1940's
Sacramento

TIE-IT-ON
1930's
Tieton

TOP CARD
1940's
Suisun

TRIANGLE
1930's
Medford

TRY ONE
1930's
San Francisco

TULIP
1920's
Yakima

VACA VALLEY
1930's
San Francisco

VALLEY
1930's
Suisun

VALLEY OF THE MOON
1930's
Sonoma

VIOLET
1930's
Yakima

W
1920's
Santa Clara

WAGON TRAIN
1940's
Medford

WELCH
1940's
Wenatchee

WENATCHEE CHIEF
1940's
Wenatchee

WENOKA
1930's
Wenatchee

WESTERN
1920's*
Wenatchee

WESTERN SHORE
1930's
Hood

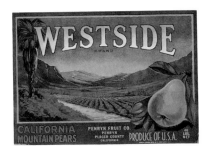

WESTSIDE
1920's*
Penryn

WEST WIND
1930's
Suisun

WINGDAM
1930's
Walnut Grove

YUBA ORCHARD
1950's
San Francisco

GRAPES

Grapes are a major California agricultural product, consumed as table grapes, raisins, and wine. While grapes are grown throughout California, table grapes are grown mainly on the east side of the San Joaquin valley in central California, in Tulare, San Joaquin, Kern, and Fresno counties. Many varieties of grapes are grown, with Thompson Seedless, Emperor, Tokay, and Malaga being of key commercial importance.

Grapes are very perishable, and require careful handling to prevent crushing. They are packed in flat lug boxes containing about 25 pounds of grapes, with labels about 13″ x 4″. Wooden boxes were used until the 1960's and gradually were replaced with cardboard boxes with wood ends, which provided more support for the contents than a box made completely of cardboard. Paper labels are still used on these boxes.

The long narrow shape of grape labels requires different design treatments than those on the relatively square labels used for other fruit boxes. Effective designs are those which feature extended lettering and elongated images.

A huge number of grape labels have been used and continue to be used. No attempt is made here to provide a complete classification; only representative examples are shown.

ABRONIA
1930's
Mecca

AIR KING
1940's
Lodi

AMERICAN EAGLE
1920's
North Dinuba

AMERICAN PRIDE
1940's
Los Angeles

ANGELINA
1940's
Acampo

A-OKAY
1950's
Los Angeles

ARENAS
1940's
Los Angeles

AUNT-JENNIE
1940's
Lindsay

BABY
1930's
Fresno

BABY MARIE
1940's
Manteca

BABY TURTLE
1930's
Modesto

BALD EAGLE
1950's
Delano

BEAR MOUNTAIN
1930's
Reedley

BEAVER
1930's
Victor

BIG STUMP
1930's
Woodlake

BLACK BEAR
1930's
Victor

BLACK JOE
1930's
Lodi

BLUEBIRD
1930's
Cutler

BLUE FLASH
1950's
Exeter

BLUE HOUND
1940's
Reedley

BLUE LUPINE
1930's
Bakersfield

BLUE RIBBON
1930's
Fresno

BOCCE
1930's
Lodi

BUENA VISTA
1950's
Lodi

CALIFORNIA BEAUTY
1930's
Modesto

CATERINA
1950's
Lodi

C.D. PRUNER
1920's
Exeter

CHATEAU
1930's
Delano

CHEROKEE
1950's
Acampo

CHUMMY
1930's
Fresno

COLLINA
1940's
Lodi

CORINTHIAN
1930's
Exeter

CORSAGE
1950's
Exeter

CORSAIR
1930's
Exeter

COUNTRY BOY
1940's
Thermal

C.R. VAN BUSKIRK
1930's
Lodi

CRY BABY
1930's
Fresno

DELANO KING
1950's
Bakersfield

DOUGHERTY
1940's
Dougherty

DROMEDARY
1930's
Minkler

EARL CROWN
1940's
San Francisco

EAST WEST
1930's
Exeter

ELBAR
1940's
Sanger

EL DON
1940's
Exeter

ELKHORN
1940's
Lodi

EMBLEM
1930's
Exeter

EMERALD BAY
1950's
Lodi

EMPEROR CITY
1940's
Exeter

E/P
1950's
Exeter

ESHCOL
1930's
Dinuba

EXETER
1930's
Exeter

EXETER LILY
1930's
Exeter

FAMIGLIA
1940's
Victor

FARMER JOHN
1940's
Indio

FAT PAK
1930's
Reedley

FLASH
1940's
Cutler

FLORITA
1950's
Visalia

FLYING E
1940's
Los Angeles

FOOTHILL MAID
1940's
Woodlake

FREMONT
1930's
Exeter

FRESNO BEST
1930's
Fresno

GIANT TREE
1940's
Woodlake

GOEHRING
1920's
Victor

GOLDEN EAGLES
1940's
Stockton

GOLDEN GATE
1950's
Exeter

GOLDEN GLOW
1950's
Los Angeles

GOLDEN TROUT
1930's
Exeter

GOLD-PAN
1930's
Sacramento

GOLD RUSH
1930's
Exeter

GOOD YEAR
1920's
Rayo

HAMILTON PAK
1940's
Reedley

HONEYBUNCH
1950's
Bakersfield

J-K
1930's
Victor

JO-AN
1940's
Stockton

JUMBO
1930's
San Francisco

KING ARTHUR
1940's
Bakersfield

KING'S PRIDE
1940's
Visalia

LADY ROWENA
1940's
Ivanhoe

LA PALOMA
1940's
Cutler

LARK
1930's
Reedley

LATIMER'S
1930's
Cucamonga

LB. STERLING
1930's
Arvin

LIBERTY BELL
1930's
Fresno

LISTEN
1920's
Cutler

LONE EAGLE
1940's
Exeter

LOOK
1940's
Cutler

LUCKY HOPPY
1940's
Lodi

LULU
1950's
Lindsay

MALAGA
1915
Newcastle

MA-MA-MIA!
1950's
Reedley

MAYFLOWER
1940's
Exeter

MECCA
1950's
Mecca

MILLION DOLLAR
1930's
Exeter

MOSES
1940's
Delano

MOTHER
1940's
Cutler

MOUNTAIN GORGE
1950's
Fresno

M & R
1940's
Lodi

MR. FRESH
1950's
Lindsay

NADCO
1950's
Visalia

NEW YORKER
1930's
Fresno

NILE
1930's
Minkler

NOB HILL
1940's
Lodi

NON STOP
1940's
Stockton

NORTHERN EAGLE
1940's
Victor

O'JACK
1940's
Del Rey

OLD IRONSIDES
1930's
Exeter

OLD MISSION
1920's
Redbanks

OLD MISSION
1930's
Redbanks

OLD VINE
1920's
Victor

O SOLE MIO
1950's
Lodi

OWL
1940's
Sacramento

PACIFIC PRIDE
1930's
San Francisco

PACIFIC PRIDE
1940's
San Francisco

PAN-AMERICAN
1950's
Edison

PEP
1940's
Visalia

PEP
1950's
Visalia

PHEASANT
1930's
Visalia

PILGRIM
1950's
Exeter

POLAR BIRD
1950's
Reedley

PRIDE OF DINUBA
1920's
North Dinuba

PROGRESS
1930's
Acampo

PURSUIT
1940's
Exeter

PUSHER
1950's
Exeter

RACE TRACK
1940's
Lodi

RAINBOW'S END
1940's
Exeter

RAYO
1920's
Delano

RAYO SUNSHINE
1940's
Rayo

RED CROWN
1920's
Fairview

RED LION
1940's
Exeter

RED ROBIN
1930's
Reedley

ROCKY HILL
1930's
Exeter

ROLL-A-LONG
1940's
Modesto

ROLLING MEADOW
1940's
Exeter

ROSE
1920's
Sanger

ROSEVILLE BELLE
1920's
Roseville

ROSY
1950's
Fresno

ROYAL FLUSH
1940's
Victor

SAILBOAT
1930's
Exeter

SALUTE
1930's
Escalon

SETTER
1940's
Exeter

7 - 11
1940's
Woodlake

SIERRA MOON
1930's
Delano

SILVER ARROW
1940's
Exeter

SILVER CLIPPER
1940's
Exeter

SILVER CUP
1930's
Exeter

SILVER TIP
1930's
Strathmore

SMALL BLACK
1930's
Escalon

SMOKE TREE
1940's
Visalia

SPITZ
1930's
Exeter

STAFFORD'S
1930's
Stafford

STAR FIRE
1950's
Exeter

SUGAR SWEET
1920's
Lodi

SUN-COLOR
1930's
San Francisco

SUN DISK
1950's
Los Angeles

SUNSET
1920's
Fresno

SUNSET
1940's
Fresno

SUNVIEW
1930's
Delano

SUTTER BUTTES
1940's
Yuba City

TABLE TREAT
1940's
Visalia

TALK O'THE TOWN
1930's
Ivanhoe

TEASER
1930's
Kettleman

THOROBREDS
1940's
San Francisco

THOROUGHBRED
1920's
Cutler

THREE BELLS
1940's
Reedley

TOP VALLEY
1940's
Exeter

TOUCHDOWN
1950's
San Francisco

TREASURE
1920's
Fresno

TRI-BORO
1950's
Lodi

TUXEDO PARK
1940's
Ducor

VALLEY BEAUTY
1930's
Lodi

VALLEY BOY
1950's
Victor

VALLEY QUEEN
1920's
Exeter

WHISTLE
1930's
Cutler

WHISTLING BOY
1940's
Stockton

WHITE HORSE
1940's
Sanger

WILLIAM TELL
1930's
Fresno

WIN
1940's
Ivanhoe

WINONA
1930's
Dinuba

WKW
1940's
Ivanhoe

YOKOHL
1930's
Exeter

FLORIDA CITRUS FRUITS

Although oranges have been grown in Florida since the 1500's when the Spanish explorers arrived, production on a large commercial scale did not begin until the early 1900's. A major expansion of the industry took place in the 1920's, during the Florida land boom. At the present time, three-quarters of the oranges grown in the United States come from Florida, along with over half the world's grapefruit.

The main citrus growing area in Florida is in the slightly elevated central part of the state, with extensions to the Indian River district on the Atlantic coast, and areas on the Gulf of Mexico. Because of Florida's humidity, citrus fruits are especially juicy. The key varieties of oranges grown are the Valencia, the Parson Brown, and the Pineapple, all of which ripen in the spring and summer.

Before the switch to cardboard boxes in the late 1950's, Florida citrus fruit was packed in nailed wooden boxes or in lightweight collapsible boxes with slats held together with wire. The original boxes were very large, holding about 90 pounds. Due to handling problems, they were replaced with boxes half the size, holding about a bushel. Even smaller boxes were occasionally used.

Florida citrus labels were relatively small, filling only the center of the box end. The most popular sizes were 9″ x 9″ and 6″ x 6″. Smaller tab-like labels, generally of less interest to collectors, were sometimes used.

Florida citrus labels have not been studied and documented as well as California labels, and only representative samples are shown here.

AMERICAN BEAUTY
1920's
Orlando

AZALEA
1940's
Jacksonville

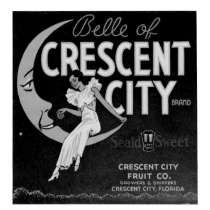

BELLE OF CRESCENT CITY
1930's
Crescent City

BEN FRANKLIN
1930's
Oviedo

BLUE AND GRAY
1930's
St. Petersburg

BLUE TIP
1930's
Winter Garden

BOOTY
1930's
Jacksonville

CARDINAL
1930's
Winter Garden

CHEST OF GOLD
1940's
St. Petersburg

CLIPPER
1920's
Frostproof

CORDIAL
1930's
Leesburg

CRESCENT MOON
1930's
Crescent City

CROWN JEWEL
1930's
Lake Wales

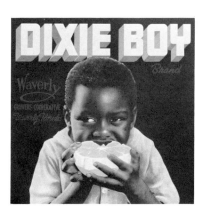

DIXIE BOY
1930's
Waverly

FELLOWSHIP
1930's
Oakland

FLO
1940's
Vero Beach

FLORIDA COWBOY
1930's
Kissimmee

FLORI GOLD
1930's
Vero Beach

FLORIGOLD GROVES
1940's
Vero Beach

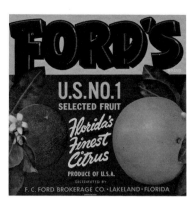

FORD'S
1950's
Lakeland

FOUR X
1930's

FULL
1930's
Waverly

GOLDEN GLO
1940's
Fort Pierce

GOLDEN HILL
1940's
Davenport

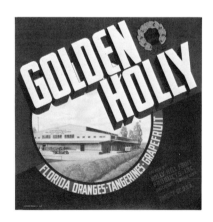

GOLDEN HOLLY
1940's
Davenport

GOLDEN SUNSET
1930's
St. Petersburg

GOOD WILL
1930's
Oakland

HUNTSMAN
1930's
Waverly

INDIAN RIVER
1930's
Ft. Pierce

JOLLY ROGER
1930's
Waverly

JUICY RIPE
1940's
Waverly

JUSTICE
1940's
Vero Beach

KEEN'S PRIDE
1930's
Frostproof

KISS-ME
1940's
Kissimmee

MAPLE LEAF
1940's
Oviedo

MERRY XMAS
1920's
Davenport

MOONBEAM
1940's
Oviedo

MOONBEAM
1930's
Oviedo

NORDEN
1940's
Lake Wales

OUR SWEETHEART
1930's
Leesburg

PEPPER
1940's
Waverly

PLEDGE
1930's
Lake County

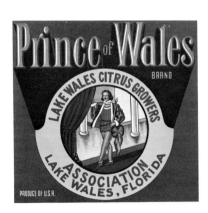

PRINCE OF WALES
1940's
Lake Wales

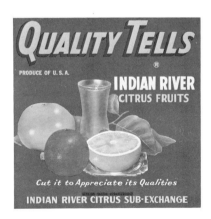

QUALITY TELLS
1940's
Vero Beach

RAZOR BACK
1930's
Frostproof

RED CLOUD
1930's
Haines City

RIDER
1930's
Eustis

RIVER GEM
1940's
Fort Pierce

RIVER ROYAL
1940's
Fort Pierce

ROYAL ARMS
1930's
Lake Wales

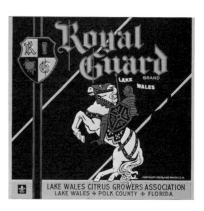

ROYAL GUARD
1940's
Lake Wales

SEALD-PEP
1930's
Waverly

SEGARI
1940's
Lake Alfred

SILVER KING
1930's
St. Petersburg

SILVER MEDAL
1930's
Sanford

SOUTH LAKE
1940's
Oakland

SUNNYSIDE
1930's
Leesburg

SUNSET HILL
1940's
San Mateo

SUNSHINE FRUITS
1930's
Miami

THRONE
1930's
Winter Garden

WAVERLY
1930's
Waverly

WHITE ROSE
1930's
Oviedo

WISE BIRD
1930's
Winter Garden

OTHER FRUITS AND VEGETABLES

California produces and ships a wide variety of fruits and vegetables in addition to the citrus fruit, apples, pears and grapes already discussed. These are grown throughout the state in regions—often originally located by trial and error—which have suitable climate, freedom from insect pests, availability of irrigation water if needed, and the capability of growing crops in off-market seasons.

Most vegetables are grown in the Watsonville-Salinas area south of San Francisco, in the Sacramento and San Joaquin River valleys, and in the Imperial and Coachella valleys in the southeastern part of the state. Winter vegetables are grown in these California desert valleys as well as, more recently, in Arizona and Texas. The most common vegetable box used for lettuce, carrots and other vegetables, is a wire-wrapped wooden box, with a tall rectangular label about 7″ x 9″. Many of the labels are general purpose; they do not specify the contents in detail.

A number of fragile products including cherries, melons, peaches, plums, and tomatoes are shipped in flat lug boxes similar to grape boxes. The long rectangular labels used on these range in size from 13″ x 5″ to 9″ x 3″.

Asparagus, grown mainly in San Joaquin county, is packed in a trapezoidal box, narrower at the top than the bottom to hold the tapering stalks of asparagus. The trapezoidal label is about 10″ x 9″.

While a gradual transition has been made to cardboard boxes, many of these products still are shipped in wooden crates, wire-wrapped wooden crates, or pressed wood boxes with paper labels or tags. The labels in current use generally have a limited advertising message, and serve only to quickly identify the contents.

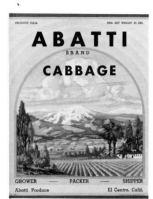

ABATTI
1940's
El Centro

BEAU GESTE
1940's
El Centro

BIG PATCH
1930's
Watsonville

BIG TOWN
1940's
Phoenix

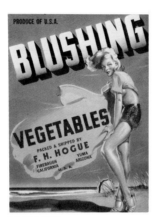

BLUSHING
1930's
Firebaugh

CARL JOSEPH
1940's
Holtville

CAROUSEL
1940's
San Jose

CHALLENGER
1940's
Guadalupe

CHEERIO
1930's
Salinas

CHOOSY
1940's
Somerton

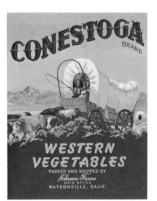

CONESTOGA
1940's
Watsonville

DOE
1940's
Holtville

DOMINATOR
1940's
Watsonville

FIREFALL
1940's
San Jose

FLYING COLORS
1940's
Watsonville

FOUR STAR
1940's
Salinas

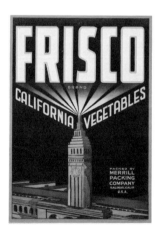

FRISCO
1930's
Salinas

GARDEN PRIZE
1940's
Holtville

GARIN-TEE
1940's
Salinas

GIANT
1930's
Salinas

GOLD HARP
1940's
Brawley

GREEN HARP
1940's
Brawley

GREEN HEAD
1940's
San Jose

GREEN PRIZE
1940's
El Centro

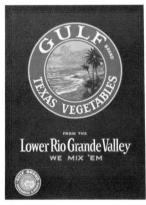

GULF
1940's
Weslaco

H H H
1950's
Santa Maria

HARDEN FARMS
1950's
Salinas

HIS NIBS
1940's
Salinas

HOT
1940's
Guadalupe

HY-TEMPO
1940's
Blythe

IRISH BEAUTY
1950's

KATHY ANNE
1950's
Watsonville

KILLER
1940's
Los Angeles

KING PELICAN
1920's
Clarksburg

KREME DE KOKE
1930's
Salinas

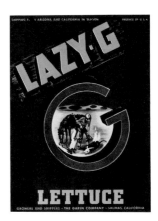

LAZY-G
1950's
Salinas

LIGO
1940's
San Francisco

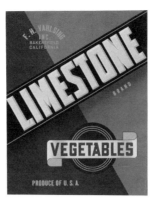

LIMESTONE
1930's
Bakersfield

LION
1930's
Watsonville

M
1940's
Salinas

MAHOGANY
1950's
Phoenix

MESA-KING
1940's
Mesa

MISTA JOE
1940's
Salinas

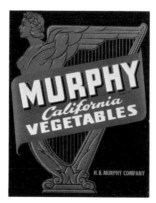

MURPHY
1950's
Brawley

MUSTANG
1950's
Guadalupe

O-GEE
1940's
Salinas

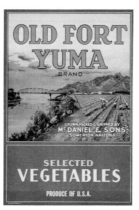

OLD FORT YUMA
1930's
Somerton

ON RUSH
1930's
Firebaugh

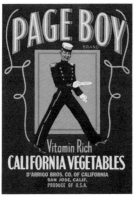

PAGE BOY
1930's
San Jose

PATRICIA
1940's
San Jose

PHELAN-FINE
1940's
Oceano

PINTO
1940's
Castroville

PLENTI GRAND
1940's
Watsonville

PURPLE SAGE
1930's
Guadalupe

RED ROOSTER
1930's
San Francisco

ROSE BRIGHT
1940's
El Centro

ROYAL BRUCE
1940's
El Centro

R R R
1950's
Phoenix

SAFE HIT
1940's
Weslaco

SANTA MARIA
1930's
Santa Maria

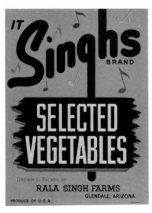

SINGHS
1950's
Glendale

SKEEZER
1950's
Salinas

SOUZA
1940's
Santa Maria

STARBOARD
1940's
Guadalupe

SUN-GROWN
1950's
Watsonville

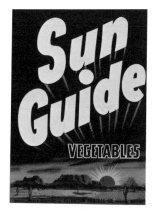

SUN GUIDE
1950's
Phoenix

TEEN-AGE
1940's
Watsonville

TOP FORM
1940's
Phoenix

TOP ROW
1930's
Watsonville

UP N'ATOM
1930's
Watsonville

VALU-PAK
1940's
Brawley

VERIGOOD
1940's
Salinas

WESTERN HOE
1950's
Salinas

WESTIE
1930's
Mesa

WHITE HOUSE
1940's
Los Angeles

STOCK LABEL
1930's

OTHER VEGETABLE LABELS

BEAR
1940's
Oceano
5" x 7"

BIG WESTERN
1940's
Guadalupe
5" x 7"

BIKINI
1950's
Oceano
5" x 7"

BLUE CROWN
1940's
El Centro
6½" x 7"

BRONCO
1940's
Castroville
9" x 9"

BRONCO BUSTER
1940's
Castroville
5" x 7"

CAL ART
1930's
Castroville
5" x 7"

CAL GEMS
1940's
Santa Maria
5" x 7"

ELKHORN
1950's
Lodi
5" x 7"

GARDEN GATE
1940's
Salinas
5" x 7"

HOT
1950's
Guadalupe
5" x 7"

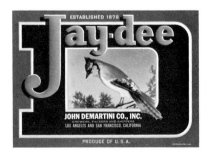

JAY-DEE
1940's
Los Angeles
5" x 7"

KING FISH
1930's
Sacramento
6" x 8"

KING PELICAN
1930's
Sacramento
5" x 7"

KING PELICAN
1930's
Sacramento
6" x 8"

LUCKY
1930's
Salinas

MARCH
1940's
Santa Maria

MAYWOOD COLONIES
1900*
Corning
6" x 9"

MISS ATWATER
1940's
Atwater
3½" x 7"

MUSTANG
1950's
Guadalupe
5" x 7"

OCEAN MIST
1930's
Castroville
9" x 9"

PHELAN-FINE
1940's
Oceano
5" x 7"

PINTO
1940's
Castroville
5" x 7"

RED COACH INN
1940's
Salinas
5" x 7"

SAFE HIT
1940's
Weslaco, Texas
5" x 7"

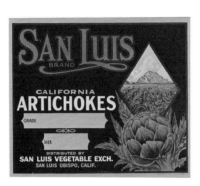

SAN LUIS
1930's
San Luis Obispo
9" x 9"

SHO-AM-SWEET
1920's
Los Angeles
8" x 9"

SHO-AM-SWEET
1930's
Los Angeles
4" x 7"

STARLET
1940's
Oceano
5" x 7"

SWEET PATOOTIE
1930's
Los Angeles
5" x 7"

ASPARAGUS LABELS

AIR KING
1960's
Lodi

CAPITAL PAK
1930's
Sacramento

CHICKIE
1950's
San Francisco

COIN
1940's
San Francisco

DITTO
1950's
Los Angeles

EARLY SPRING
1940's
Stockton

GOLD CUP
1940's
Stockton

HI-GOAL
1940's
Salinas

KING FISH
1930's
Sacramento

KING O'HEARTS
1940's
Salinas

KING'S CADETS
1930's
Clarksburg

LONG GREEN
1950's
Stockton

LUCKY SELLER
1950's
San Francisco

MAGGIO
1940's*
Lodi

MAGIC
1940's
Middle River

OH YES!
1950's
San Francisco

PRIDE OF THE RIVER
1930's
Sacramento

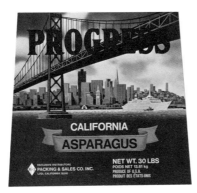

PROGRESS
1960's
Lodi

RED ROOSTER
1930's
San Francisco

RIVER LAD
1930's
Fullerton

RIVER MAID
1930's
Lodi

SKY PATH
1950's
San Francisco

SPRING IS HERE!
1940's
Stockton

TALK OF THE TOWN
1950's
San Francisco

STOCK LABEL
1950's

LUG BOX LABELS

BRANDT
1940's
Reedley
4" x 13"

BUNGALOW
1940's
Turlock
6" x 13"

BUTTE
1930's
Hamilton City
4" x 11"

BUXOM
1940's
Firebaugh
4" x 10"

CAL-HEART
1940's
Turlock
6" x 13"

CALIFORNIA CHERRIES
1930's
Sacramento
3" x 9"

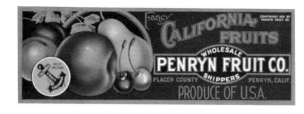

CALIFORNIA FRUITS
1920's
Penryn
4" x 11"

C. MAGGIO
1950's
Lodi
4" x 12"

COLFAX FRUIT
1920's
Colfax
4" x 11"

CORVETTE
1940's
Stockton
3" x 10"

DOMINATOR
1940's
Watsonville
5" x 13"

EKCO
1930's
Turlock
6" x 13"

FANTASIA
1940's
Fresno
5" x 13"

5 POINTS
1940's
Five Points
4" x 10"

42ND STREET
1940's
Yuba City
5" x 13"

GOLDEN BEAR
1940's
Mills
4" x 13"

GOOD MORNING
1930's
Delano
4" x 10"

HI-COLOR
1940's
San Francisco
3" x 11"

HIGH HAND
1920's
Loomis
2" x 9"

HONEY BEE
1940's
Reedley
4" x 13"

JO JO
1940's
Somerton
4" x 9"

JU-C
1930's
Westmorland
4" x 11"

KERNEL KORN
1940's
Los Angeles
4" x 13"

KING CROW
1940's
Crows Landing
4" x 10"

K O
1950's
Cutler
4" x 13"

LE GRAND
1940's
Le Grand
5" x 13"

LIVE OAK
1930's
Le Grand
6" x 13"

LO BUE'S
1940's
San Jose
3" x 10"

MISS GIFFEN
1950's
Huron
6" x 14"

NINO
1940's
Los Angeles
4" x 13"

OUR STATE
1930's
San Francisco
5" x 13"

PACIFIC PRIDE
1930's
San Francisco
4" x 13"

PEACOCK
1940's
Turlock
6" x 14"

PIGEON
1940's
Modesto
4" x 13"

PILIBOS
1940's
Fresno
4" x 10"

PREVO
1950's
La Mesa
4" x 13"

PRINCE
1930's
Orange Cove
4" x 13"

RED WAGON
1940's
Reedley
4" x 13"

ROSEBUD
1930's
Strathmore
4" x 13"

SARATOGA
1940's
San Jose
5" x 13"

SILVER TIP
1930's
Strathmore
4" x 13"

SUTTER BUTTES
1940's
Yuba City
4" x 12"

SWALLOW
1930's
Woodlake
4" x 13"

TEXUS
1940's
Weslaco
5" x 13"

TULARE CHIEF
1940's
Cutler
4" x 13"

WESTWARD HO
1940's
Pheonix
4" x 11"

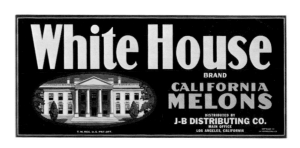

WHITE HOUSE
1940's
Los Angeles
6" x 14"

STOCK LABEL
1930's
6" x 14"

STOCK LABEL
1930's
4" x 11"

Loading cantaloupes into refrigerated railroad cars.
Brawley, California, about 1920.

LABEL COLLECTIONS, ARTICLES, AND EXHIBITIONS

Interest in fruit box labels as collectable items has increased greatly in the past few years, as their artistic and historical qualities have been recognized. Many people are assembling major collections, newspaper and magazine articles appear regularly, and several exhibitions in museums and art galleries have been held.

PUBLIC LABEL COLLECTIONS

Bowers Museum, Santa Ana, California
Huntington Library, San Marino, California
Kunstbibliothek, Berlin, Germany
Museum of Florida History, Tallahassee, Florida
Pomona Public Library, Pomona, California
Riverside Museum, Riverside, California
Riverside Public Library, Riverside, California
Sherman Foundation, Corona del Mar, California
University of California (Library Special Collections), Davis, California
University of California (Library Special Collections), Fullerton, California
University of California (Library Special Collections), Berkeley, California
University of Wyoming (School of American Studies), Laramie, Wyoming

MAGAZINE ARTICLES

Over 50 newspaper and magazine articles have been written on the subjects of label history and label collecting. The most important among these include:
Westways (September, 1969)
Look Magazine (August, 1971)
Acquire Magazine (October, 1974)
New Times (July, 1976)
California Historical Quarterly (Spring, 1977)
American Heritage (April, 1977)
Changing Times (June, 1983)
Collector's Showcase (December, 1983)

BOOKS

Orange Crate Art, By John Salkin and Laurie Gordon (Warner Books, 1976).
The Encyclopedia of Collectables (Time-Life Books, Inc. 1978) Volume 7, pp. 30-45. Discusses and illustrates a variety of fruit box labels.

MUSEUM AND GALLERY EXHIBITIONS

Museum of Science and Industry, Los Angeles, California (1970)
Galerie Mikro, Berlin, Germany (1972, 1973)
Cooper House Gallery, Santa Cruz, California (1974)
Kinsman-Morrison Gallery, London, England (1974)
Whitney Museum, New York, New York (1974)
Harnell College, Salinas, California (1976)
California Historical Society, San Francisco, California (1976)
Vincent van Gogh Museum, Amsterdam, Netherlands (1976)
M.H. De Young Museum, San Francisco, California (1976)
Sunderland Art Centre, England (1976)
Museum of the Rockies, Bozeman, Montana (1977)
Oregon State University, Corvallis, Oregon (1977)
Oakland Museum, Oakland, California (1977)
Southern Oregon State College, Ashland, Oregon (1977)
University of California, Santa Barbara, California (1977)
University of North Carolina, Charlotte, North Carolina (1977)
Bank of America Corporation Gallery, San Francisco, California (1978)
The Rotunda, Baltimore, Maryland (1978)
University of California, Fullerton, California (1978 and 1982)
Wells-Fargo Museum, San Francisco, California (1979)
Dartmouth College, Dartmouth, New Hampshire (1979)
Grange Gallery, Toronto, Canada (1980)
Great Western Savings Gallery, San Francisco, California (1982)

This book is an initial attempt to categorize and illustrate the subject of fruit box labels. Comments and suggestions regarding labels which should be included in future editions, and general questions regarding label collecting should be directed to the authors, Hillcrest Press, Inc., P.O. Box 10636, Beverly Hills, California, 90210.

INDEX

(A) Apples

(F) Cherries, plums, peaches, etc.

(FC) Florida citrus fruit

(G) Grapes

(GF) Grapefruit

(L) Lemons

(M) Melons

(O) California oranges

(P) Pears

(V) Vegetables

–H–

0116

1-8-92 Midwest 17.95 48113